# My State MAINE

By Christina Earley

## TABLE OF CONTENTS

Maine.............................3
Glossary.........................22
Index............................24

A Crabtree Seedlings Book

Crabtree Publishing
crabtreebooks.com

# School-to-Home Support for Caregivers and Teachers

This book helps children grow by letting them practice reading. Here are a few guiding questions to help the reader build his or her comprehension skills. Possible answers appear in red.

## Before Reading:

- What do I know about Maine?
  - *I know that Maine is a state.*
  - *I know that there are many lighthouses in Maine.*

- What do I want to learn about Maine?
  - *I want to learn which famous people were born in Maine.*
  - *I want to learn what the state flag looks like.*

## During Reading:

- What have I learned so far?
  - *I have learned that Augusta is the state capital of Maine.*
  - *I have learned that the Maine coastline is 3,478 miles (5,597 km) long.*

- I wonder why...
  - *I wonder why the state flower is the white pinecone.*
  - *I wonder why so many sailing ships were built in Bath.*

## After Reading:

- What did I learn about Maine?
  - *I have learned that you can fish on the Allagash Wilderness Waterway.*
  - *I have learned that the state animal is the moose.*

- Read the book again and look for the glossary words.
  - *I see the word* ***capital*** *on page 6, and the word* ***skiing*** *on page 21. The other glossary words are found on pages 22 and 23.*

# MAINE

Hi! My name is Iris. Welcome to Maine!

I live in Bath. My city is known as the City of Ships because of all the sailing ships that were built here.

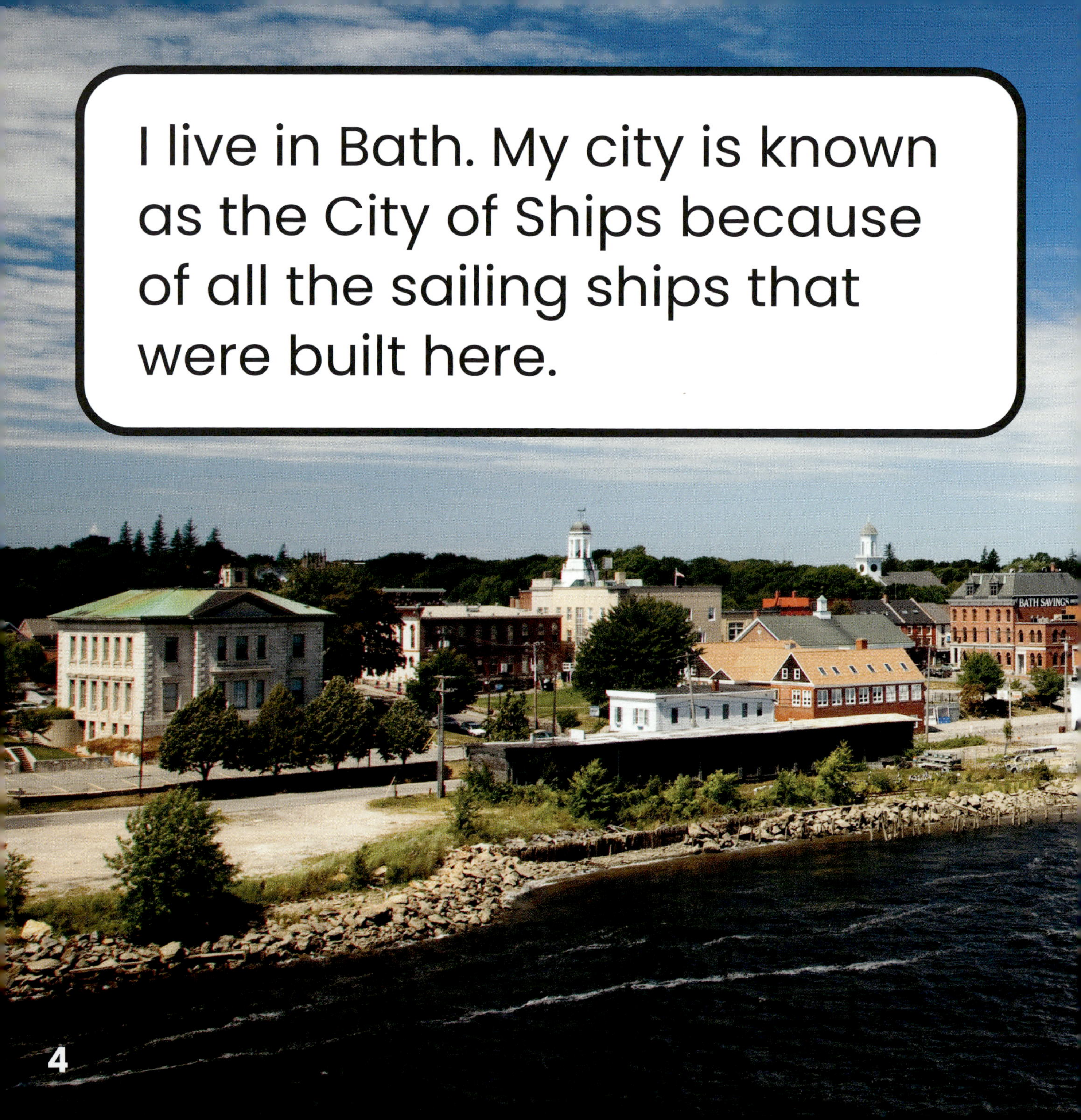

There are many **historic** buildings in Bath. Visiting my city is like traveling back in time!

Maine is in the northeastern United States. The **capital** is Augusta.

Fun Fact: Portland is the largest city in Maine.

The state animal is the **moose**.

The white pinecone is the state flower.

We catch a lot of lobster in Maine. Some of it is used to make **lobster rolls**.

Fun Fact: Maine fishers catch about 108 million pounds (49 million kg) of lobster a year.

My state flag is blue. The state **coat of arms** is in the middle.

The Portland Sea Dogs baseball games are fun to watch.

I like to go boating on the Atlantic Ocean. Sometimes we see whales.

Fun Fact: The entire coastline of Maine is 3,478 miles (5,597 km) long!

I enjoy backpacking in Acadia National Park.

My family rides the Ferris wheel at Old Orchard Beach.

Author Stephen King was born in Maine. Actress and dancer Victoria Rowell was also born in Maine.

Fun Fact: Vice President Hannibal Hamlin was born in Paris Hill, Maine.

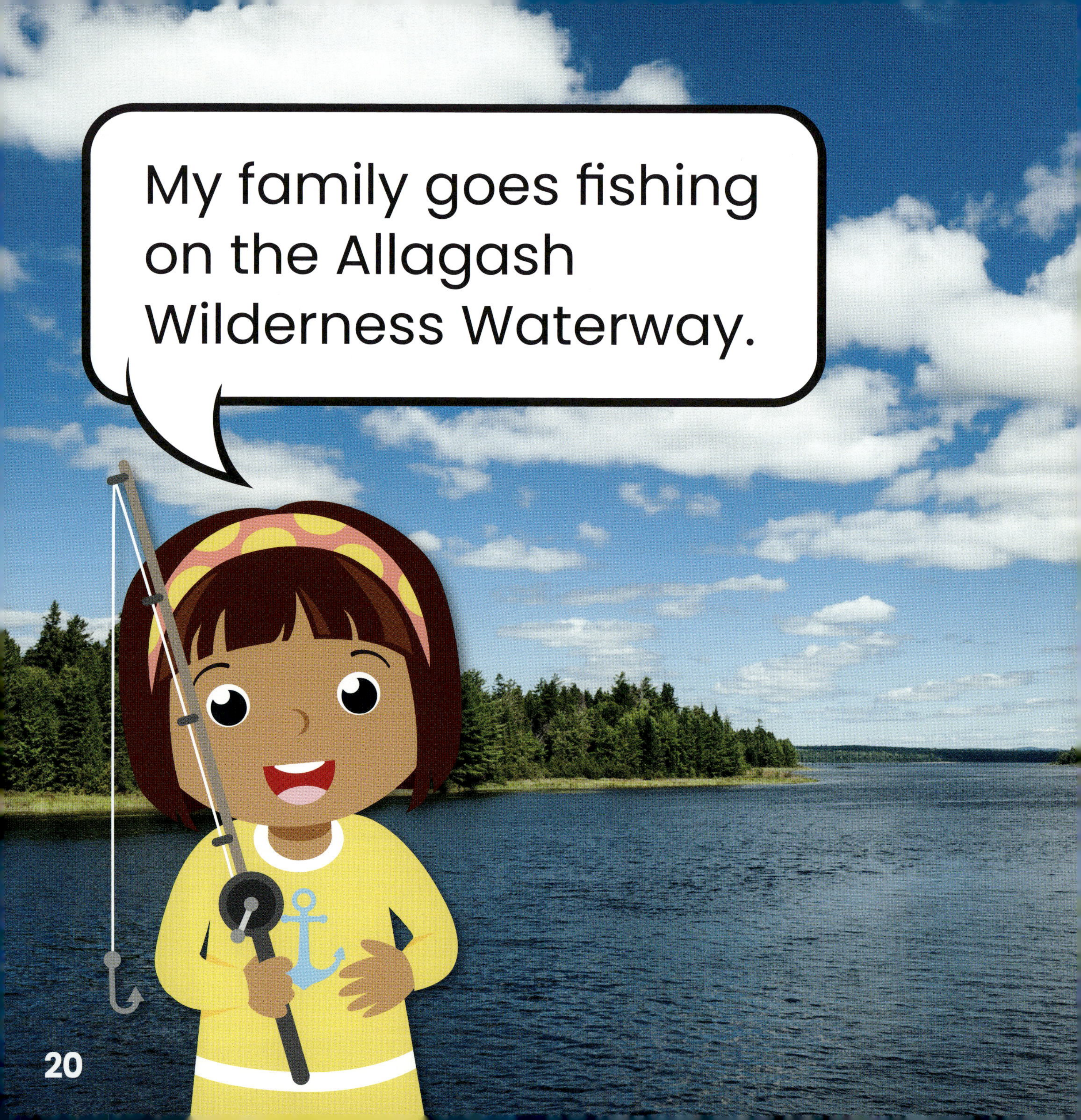
My family goes fishing on the Allagash Wilderness Waterway.